RESTORING MASCULINITY AFTER SEPARATION

RESTORING MASCULINITY AFTER SEPARATION

Becoming the Better Man

LUIS
OTERO JR

Outskirts Press, Inc.
Denver, Colorado

I dedicate this book to the person whom helped transform my perception of myself following broken relationships. After a lost summer of wallowing in self-pity, she grabbed me by the collar and challenged me to WAKE THE HELL UP! Since that day, I uncovered the better aspects of my being that I kept hidden because my **self-pity became comfortable.** I elicit now a more confident self, enabling more success in relationships and completing projects (such as this book) that I would have only dreamed of and never attempted. For pushing me to be better, Kori, I appreciate you from the bottom of my heart, shukran habibty.

Table of Contents

Purpose

I WROTE THIS book as a guide for fellow divorced men who find themselves perhaps at middle age and as newly single. Multitudes of emotions and insecurities develop about where life will take men and how they can begin new relationships with women. This by no means is a 'pick-up' type of book, and I have purposely eschewed the PUA (pick-up artist) lexicon because I believe the better man views and treats women as human beings. The opinions and discussion herein will concentrate on how a man empowers himself and demonstrates the BEST side of his personality from power WITHIN.

We are bombarded with messages on how men should behave toward women and relationships, and more often than not, this leads to confusion that is detrimental for the man. Life provides a plethora of experiences and a man may not 'win' every interaction. **A man is defeated when he refuses to learn how to bounce back after challenging situations.**

Learning from our defeats results in much better character and a stronger, confident man. I have detailed my personal struggles with life and all of the preconceptions, misconceptions, and insecurities I carried with me as well as the mistakes

I made along the way. Throughout the book I outlined some methods I learned to better manage MYSELF. This, however, is a continuous, life-learning process that the better man contemplates and evaluates until he returns to the Creator.

Of utmost importance is the relationship a man has with his children. My children are my world. A man's children are the number one priority regardless of what other female companions a man may encounter along the way. **THIS CANNOT BE UNDERSTATED**.

1

Chance Meeting

IN CALIFORNIA, PROSPECTIVE teachers complete a series of tests to prove proficiency in different subject areas before earning their teaching credential. I teach a class that prepares them for the first of those tests, the California Basic Education Standards Test (CBEST). I taught the class for seven years at the Los Angeles County Office of Education (LACOE). However due to the recession and low enrollment, classes had been canceled for the previous six months. Finally in the spring of 2009*, the class was on. I didn't expect anything different than had been the case in the previous seven years. At the time, I was divorced after 14 years of marriage.

"Hi, I'm Early." I gazed at the door and suddenly became enthralled by a vision I never expected nor had seen before. I immediately replied "Hello Early, I'm Luis". We shared a quick laugh and I stood stunned by the beautiful light green eyes and flowing curly hair that stood in facing me.

"Oh yes, my name is Yasmeen*," she said as we shook hands, and I purposely held on to her hand for a longer instance. My eyes would not wander away from her eyes, locked into position and fascinated by the juxtaposition of her eyes to her abundantly flowing curly hair. Thank goodness she was "early" so I had a chance to flirt, I mean chat, with her before other students walked in.

- Information has been changed to protect the subject's identity.

She had a key around her neck that read 'Jordan' and had its flag on it. I found out she was born in Jordan and had moved to Norwalk, CA when she was 12 years old. Most of her family lived in Palmdale, CA about an hour from downtown Los Angeles. As a Christian I knew about Jordan and its importance in the Bible, but I had never met anyone from there. She was the first Arab woman I met since I hired a nineteen-year old Egyptian at my previous job 13 years earlier. Yasmeen's striking green eyes, curly hair and confident demeanor immediately attracted me. She wanted to take the math portion of the class, so I would only see her for class that Friday night and Saturday morning. Come to think of it, her name wasn't even on the registration list, but I was so entranced by those eyes, I don't ever remember registering her properly for the class. Oops. Throughout the evening, I tried to keep my eyes off of her eyes as she sat right in the front of the class. I noticed that she responded with flirty gazes and smiles too. This proved the toughest math class I had to teach and for some reason, I felt that the whole class stared at both of us. I searched for Yasmeen during the break but she slipped out to get something to eat. Damn, a missed opportunity. After the break, though, flirty glances and smiles continued. I tried as much as possible to concentrate but needless to say my concentration was broken. At one point, I refused to look in her direction, but I felt those laser beam eyes on me. I asked her questions (about the math of course) to ensure I seized the opportunity to talk to her. She continued to oblige with a wink and a hand comb of her curly hair. Wow! The four-hour class flew by way too quickly. I searched for Yasmeen the minute I dismissed class only to find her seat *empty*. Double damn, another missed opportunity.

Classes on Saturday morning begin at 8:30am. I arrived there 'early' so I could prepare. It was 8:35am when she arrived and she wore a traditional Arab dress and jeans underneath. This time I noticed she carried a coffee cup with pictures on it. I tried my best to stretch my eyes to see who was in those pictures. I noticed a boy and a girl and a MAN. Crap, my hopes were crushed. The man appeared older and heavier than Yasmeen so I prayed it was her father. I then spotted on her left hand a WEDDING RING. Double crap. I never strayed away from those striking green eyes during the first session long enough to notice a ring. At that point, now feeling all is lost, I decided to take a 'whatever' stance, it had been a terrific first flirting day so I decided to continue the flirtation and resigned myself to never see her again when the class was over. Who cares? Besides class was over at 12:30pm and I had a 2:00pm lunch date anyway. Class began normally, she sat in the front row and the glances, gazes, winks and flirtation were on. On that day, I was teaching probability so I asked:

"Do you have a quarter I may borrow"?

She glanced at me and slowly replied, "why of course." Ahh. I concluded that while she may leave me forever, I would pursue someone like her in the future, a person entirely different than I had previously experienced. At the break this time, she stayed in class, so I took the opportunity to converse. Of course, I was interrupted by other students whom had questions for me. Finally, I was able to make my way over to her area. She pretended to have questions on particular math problems so this 'gave me the excuse' to converse with her. We chatted a little and I learned that she had 2 children, one boy and one girl and had been married for eight years, but implied that things "were at rock bottom". I grabbed her coffee cup and looked at the pictures of her family. While turning the coffee cup, I admitted to her, "I can't keep my eyes off of your eyes." She replied, "neither can I." I joked to her "really are you looking in a mirror?" We both started laughing and she gave me a flirtatious punch. Then I looked at the clock and oops, break was over five minutes ago. Time to go back to teaching. I handed the students a final exam and had written a note at my desk that read "please stay after". One problem. I attempted numerous times to slip the note to her, only to have other students look up or raise their hand for me to assist with questions. I could not let this opportunity slip by again, however, time was running out. I reviewed all the problems on the test, still with the note in my pocket. Afterward class dismissed about 12:20pm and I had three students at my desk asking me questions. I noticed she began packing slowly, but we happened to meet eyes. She nodded her head and waited. Whew! I would get a final chance to talk with her and then she would leave me for good. As we sat next to each other after class, we talked about an array of subjects some serious and others not-so-serious. She admitted to taking the CBEST previously but scored too low on the math section to receive a passing grade. Also, she wanted to take the class six months ago, but became frustrated because the class had been canceled numerous times. I'm glad she waited patiently for the class to be on. Our conversation continued smoothly laughing and joking. The conversation flowed so well; we seemed to instinctively know how to react to each other. It felt as though we had always known each other and I didn't even notice the time. It was now 2:20pm, and oops, I missed my 2:00pm lunch date. This was a conversation I desired to continue well into the afternoon, but I reluctantly attempted to excuse myself. I shook her hand and lowered my voice to her "it was my pleasure to meet you, please email me and let me know how you scored."

Our hands stayed locked together for a longer period of time as we stared longingly into each other's eyes. She stood silently, her eyes attached to mine. I then pulled back and decided to give her a deep, warm hug, an act I could treasure. As I pulled back from the hug, her hand remained firmly on my back. So... I KISSED her and she responded immediately clutching me closer to her, lips pressing, tongue swirling, bodies hugging warmly. We kissed passionately for ten minutes, but I heard the security guard walking the hall way as we were the only two left in the building. I quickly lead her into the large storage closet attached to the class and we continued the passion for another 20 minutes, as my phone vibrated from incoming calls. She kissed deliciously. After we came up for air, she looked at me and said, "I really have to go." I agreed and pleaded with her not to let this be the last time we see each other. She looked up at me and said, "we could meet tonight, this *is* my night out." After exchanging information, we decided to meet at a local restaurant later that night. As we waited for our table, I asked her if she wanted a drink. Yasmeen said she doesn't drink because she is Muslim and it is against her religion. Another shocker because I had never been with a Muslim before and given the media blitz after 9/11, she was supposed to be the 'enemy'. However, there I stood with her interlocking lips. Holy crap what was I getting into, the feeling, though, incredible. She proved a wealth of knowledge and information, with her education outside the United States and the fact she could speak Arabic, French,

Spanish and English. Talk about a *turn on*. We skipped the restaurant and decided instead to visit the local coffee shop. The coffee maker greeted us and asked "what could I start for you today?" I replied under my breath "a war". She burst out laughing since a few minutes earlier we had discussed this particular shop and "war". An amazing evening developed as I morphed into the student that night, a woman 12 years younger than me becoming the teacher describing her worldly experiences. The night ended with passionate embraces and a promise to continue again. I learned what I had always believed, information presented by our politicians and the media (and other people for that matter) should be scrutinized and not trusted at face value. Base opinions on your own experiences with other people and do not be influenced by *the lie machine*. I felt like Christopher Columbus, I 'discovered a new world' (which had already been here).

But seriously, what the hell was I doing?

2

The "Relationship"

IT WAS NOW Sunday morning and I woke up energized from a whirlwind evening. I received a text that morning from Yasmeen. She had just awakened and was sneaking in a text. I asked her to teach me a few words of Arabic since I became fascinated about the thought of learning something new. The first two words she taught me in Arabic were "eshtetelak" which she said means "I miss you" and "bahebak" which means "I love you" (I am using transliteration here and not proper Arabic script). I couldn't believe those were the first two words she taught me. Did that mean anything significant? Our texts ended right away because the kids and her husband were awake now. It wasn't until around 10:30pm that I received a call from Yasmeen. She lay in bed while her husband watched television in the living room. She related how terribly her day went and how she desired to see me. She tired of how badly her husband treated her and how their relationship progressed to such a low point. Yasmeen expressed dissatisfaction as well with some of the cultural expectations in her marriage. I did not have knowledge of what those were and if those expectations were any different than my experience with American expectations of marriage and relationships.

It was now Monday morning, driving to my regular teaching job as a 7th grade history teacher, I received a call from Yasmeen, she was a teacher's aide for L.A. Unified School District and was also driving to work. I could hear her kids in the background, singing and talking as young children do. She was about to drop them off, when she asked, "can we see each other tonight?" I gladly said "yes" and she confidently replied "good we'll work out the details later."

As the day progressed, I had that churning feeling inside my stomach, I felt strong attraction, but I am not supposed to feel that way because of her situation. How the hell do I handle the situation, but more importantly, *how do I handle how I feel?* Yasmeen and I talked later that afternoon, she usually gets the kids to bed around 8pm, then she will "go to the store" and meet me downstairs from her place. HOLY CRAP! That night she entered my van, both of us in the front seats. I wanted to talk with her but upon sitting down she said "Can we go back there?" I was trying to play it cool, but nobody has to ask me twice!

More texts and phone conversations continued. I received a "happy birthday" call from Yasmeen, which was a terrific surprise since I had told her only once when my birthday was. She asked me what I had planned and I replied that I was meeting friends for happy hour. She said, "if you are done early, meet me, I have a *present* for you."

A couple of weeks later I received an additional surprise. After one of her texts she wrote 'eshtetelak' and 'bahebak'. I remained stunned as I reread the text message. I wondered if that's why she taught me those words earlier. I understood what the words meant but I fumbled with the phone not knowing how to respond. This relationship seemed to progress rather quickly, however, I felt the same way. Yasmeen courageously took that first step. We talked again that night and she related to me that she had a previously planned summer vacation to Jordan and would be gone for nearly three months. She said she now regretted going but she so missed her country. Her plan was to return by the end of August in time to register the kids for school. Wow, what a tangled web we weave, an unbelievable whirlwind experience, but now it was toward the end of April and we only had six weeks before she departed. Moreover, we had talked so much during the first three weeks that I had to give her my second line phone to keep the costs down. I had now fallen deeply for her but *how do I handle my feelings?*

During the first week of May, Yasmeen took me to a different Mediterranean restaurant than the one we had frequented. This one was Gitana Mediterranean Cuisine in Burbank, CA., about 10 minutes north from downtown Los Angeles. That night we met our server, Kori. She seemed irritated at Yasmeen for wanting her water with lots of lemon and mint. Yasmeen caught me looking at Kori (oops), but I quickly covered it by saying, "she's pretty but her attitude sucks." We ate something I never had before 'chicken shawarma', which tasted delicious. Yasmeen also smoked hookah; she tried to introduce it to me previously but I weakly tried it a few times. I had never smoked *anything* before (what a nerd). On this occasion, I decided to try a few puffs but I ended up coughing and choking. I remember hearing Kori repeat under her breath as she walked away, "amateur!" How embarrassing. After a few more sessions, I finally got the hang of smoking hookah. "Hey," Yasmeen said surprised that I didn't immediately give her the hookah pipe back, "now I've created a monster and I have to share?" Her eyes sparkled as she witnessed my satisfaction with finally being able to completely share an activity she thoroughly enjoyed. Another time at Gitana, Yasmeen introduced me to a traditional Jordanian dance 'dabke'. I was totally taken off guard. As soon the song came on, she grabbed my hand and we ended up joining a circle of other dabke enthusiasts. I had no clue what I was doing, I kicked my leg up took steps to the right, kicked my leg up again…What I remember was that I was horrible at it, but again I endeavored to learn something new that was part of her culture.

As a seventh grade history teacher in California part of the standards is to teach about Arabia and the rise of Islam in the Middle Ages. However, to actually to sit down with someone from that culture and learn the different aspects of that culture became a worthwhile experience for me. I was the student asking questions so I may comprehend the culture better and, in turn, pass that new knowledge to my students. Yasmeen willingly taught me about Arabic language, music and culture. Talk about hands-on learning! Yasmeen told me an interesting story about her family. She related that her uncle used to work for a man named Salem Bin Laden. Now I laughed and told her that it couldn't be 'that' Salem Bin Laden but apparently she wasn't kidding. I answered "You know, I had always heard that everyone in the world is 5 Degrees of Separation from everyone else, so that would be put me 5 Degrees of Separation from another famous Bin Laden…" Who knew?

Time was running out for me. It's about two weeks until she leaves for Jordan. I had already fallen deeply for her, repeating "bahebak" to her and she to me. I certainly did not look forward to the calendar changing to June. The two months we were together seemed to fly at the speed of light, not a dull moment and I couldn't even remember the time before I met her. I could only lament the fact that there would be a long break for us until she returned, that was the original plan. How would I handle the time when she is gone? Would I continue to meet other women in the meantime, or would I wait? What about her, perhaps she would be separated by the time of her return, so what could that mean for us? It was further complicated because of our different religious beliefs, not really for me but for *her*. Our relationship was never about our faiths; we had discussed our differences only one time. Our relationship was only about the love Yasmeen and I shared. I guess her time away would be the ultimate test. How would we end up?

3

Good Bye

I HAD SEEN Yasmeen for a couple of hours at Gitana the night before her trip. I felt elated that she was able to squeeze in time for me even though her family was back at her place getting everything ready for the next day. We had talked about me seeing her off at the airport, but I wasn't sure if I wanted to with such a complicated matter and her family being there. As we parted she handed me my cell phone back; it was tough for me to accept.

D-Day. Yasmeen sent me a text early that morning at 5:00am telling me she had been up most of the night. She wanted me to go to the airport to see her off. This would prove to be the toughest good-bye ever. I told her I would wear my Dallas Cowboys jersey so I could be easily recognizable and she would wear a 'New York' shirt I had given her.

Here's the situation: Her whole family would be at the airport including her soon-to-be ex-husband to help Yasmeen and her kids board the plane. Given the nature of our 'relationship', I had never met anyone in her family, I knew of them from the many conversations we had about our families and from the pictures she had shared with me. There would be no way in hell I would be able to approach her for a hug, kiss or even a handshake good-bye. So there I stood *right next to her family* to ensure she would see me. We met eyes numerous times and smiled to each other, but it took every ounce of restraint that I had in my body not to run over there and give her a hug. What a difficult experience, the longest two hours ever. I pretended to talk on the phone, checked flights, did anything to make it look as though I was not there for her. Not that anyone would recognize me. As she entered the checkpoint to the escalator, I felt so empty. The whirlwind relationship I enjoyed so much was now coming to a sudden, heart-stopping halt.

When she reached the top of the escalator, Yasmeen looked back with her children and waved good-bye to her family. Then Yasmeen made a half-turn, faced me and waved good-bye. At least she acknowledged my presence but my heart sunk to the ground, I did not get a chance to give a proper send off, at least a hug good-bye. Though I had a close parking spot, the walk back to the car felt as if I had parked miles away. I tried one last thing, I called her and she picked up right before the plane began its taxi onto the runway. I had a final chance to hear her voice as we said "bahebak" and "eshtetelak" to each other. Then she had to hang up.

On the way home, the emptiness grew and my mind raced with thousands of thoughts, my stomach churned with feelings of anxiousness and despair. I already missed her. How would I fill up my time now? I had plenty of distractions since I taught summer school all day long and coached three soccer teams for my kids. However, I wouldn't be distracted enough. I walked around in a daze those first few days, I even sent her email messages everyday, knowing she may not be able to read them for a few days given the long trip and jet lag.

Imagine, a man as experienced as I am and *I didn't know how to control my feelings.*

On the fourth day, I received a call from an unfamiliar number and I decided to pick it up. IT WAS YASMEEN! She said she still felt jet lagged but she was happy to visit her home again. I finally had the chance to hear from her, the call lasted a few minutes but it didn't matter, I felt incredible and for the first time, I slept soundly that night. The next day, I decided to visit Gitana by myself, somehow I would feel closer to her since this was a place we frequented. That night I sat in Kori's section, she had been our regular server.

Kori asked "Hey, where's your girlfriend?" I told her that she was spending the summer in Jordan.

"Hmm, this is a big test for you" Kori said.

"Yes, we'll see what happens when or IF she comes back", I replied.

We actually had a pleasant conversation something we had not really done before. I felt comfortable that night, I brought some magazines to read while I smoked hookah *by myself* this time. If I did it once, I could do it again.

On Father's Day, I spent a terrific day with the kids at the beach and then the pool. As I lay in bed tired from the sun and all the activities, I received another call from an unfamiliar number, but this time I recognized it as an international call. YASMEEN! She called to wish me a happy Father's Day and we ended up talking for nearly an hour. Wow, what a great end to the day. This new number would be hers and since there was a ten-hour time difference, we could only talk at certain times. Sometimes we would have to talk after midnight California time, other days it would have to be at 7:00am. But no matter, hearing her voice was cathartic for me.

I continued to visit Gitana's once a week always sitting in Kori's section. We talked a great deal now and developed a friendship. She is always fun to talk to and Kori is quite insightful. I found out she was completing her master's degree in psychology and looking into investing in business ventures. She suggested that I not call Yasmeen too much because she would appreciate that I let her go and enjoy her time in Jordan. Kori said if I tried to call and email her all the time, I would come off as being *too needy*. Her honesty with me struck a great chord with me. My reasons for going to Gitana changed as the visits were now more about talking to Kori rather than going to feel close to Yasmeen, even though I missed her tremendously. This was a harbinger of the way Kori would affect the way I perceived aspects of myself in the near future.

It was now the middle of July about halfway through the time Yasmeen would be gone. I called her and she was in the doctor's office.

"Are you ok, what happened?" I inquired nervously.

"I'm fine, its just a routine check-up" Yasmeen said.

The doctor was on his way in so she hung up. Still, I was worried about her because she had visited the doctor a number of times during our time together for a number of different ailments.

I called Yasmeen the next day at 7:00am California time before I had to go to work to find out how her appointment went. I WAS NOT READY FOR HER ANSWER.

"How was the doctor's appointment, are you ok? I asked.

"It went fine, hey guess what, I got a job", Yasmeen replied.

She kept talking but I did not hear anything else she said, her voice had the same muffling sound as Charlie Brown's teacher. A million thoughts ran through my mind.

"So you're not coming back are you?" I inquired.

Yasmeen replied that it was a temporary job, she needed some money; however, the advertising position she accepted did not sound temporary at all. Then it made sense to me why she was at the doctor's office the day before. I couldn't understand, but really I didn't want to understand. Yasmeen said she had to do it for herself and it was nothing about me, but all the while, I could only think to myself if I was the one that drove her to stay there. The emptiness I now felt was 100 times greater than when I had left the airport.

I entered the classroom that morning with a fogged mind; the whole day at work was a blur. Between classes and all during lunch I could not fathom the information Yasmeen told me that morning. Despite the fact that my soccer teams had won their games that night, the fog in my mind returned as soon as the games were over. All the fantasies I dreamed up and counting of the days for her return didn't matter anymore. I knew in my heart Yasmeen was not coming back. I had always suspected it was a realistic possibility that she would stay, but I didn't want to believe it happened for real. So many thoughts ran through my head. Did she use me to get over her husband? Did she really mean it when she said "eshtetelak" and "bahebak"? Did I enter a 'rebound relationship'? Was I just trying to enter an impossible relationship given our different faiths? My mind flooded with confusion, pity and anger.

A few days passed and I returned to Gitana. I saw Kori there.

"Have you heard from your girl?" Kori asked.

I held back every last tear in my eyes as I weakly mumbled to her "She's staying".

Kori stepped up to me, gave me a hug and whispered:

"She's stupid for staying over there and leaving you here, if she actually loved you she would have stepped up." Usually, I drove to Gitana once a week, however, this time I went there five straight days, in a sad and gloomy atmosphere feeling like such a loser. It was a struggle to keep up the charade of happiness. I had to put up the front with my family, in class and with the soccer teams. Enjoying the summer with my children and talking to Kori kept my sanity during this time. Obviously, I couldn't talk her ear off because she was working, but just knowing that she was there to listen when she could felt extremely comforting for me. I spent the rest of summer thoroughly dazed and introverted. A married couple whom are friends of mine tried to set me up with their friend but it didn't work out. I just wasn't into meeting any new dating partners. In retrospect, I came off so weak and needy that this new girl ended up *running* back to her ex. I felt so pitiful, I kept to myself most of the time, and if I went out, it was only to Gitana to read and talk to Kori. I didn't feel like meeting anyone because I was not confident in my ability to handle my feelings again and I felt miserable about *myself*. The rest of the summer remained the same, after having fun with the kids all day long, I stayed alone purposely.

4

Kori

AS USUAL SUMMERTIME flew by quickly as it was now toward the end of August. I *had been* feeling better about myself lately after having gone on vacation with the kids to Las Vegas and the river for a week. However, I discovered something I wished I had just thrown away earlier. I found a copy of Yasmeen's itinerary she had given me. To make matters worse, I found it on the day she was supposed to return. I could not believe I was dealt such cruel and twisted fate. Just after I had been feeling a tiny bit more confident about myself, now all of the confusion, pity and anger returned.

Too many questions confused my mind. Why had we met in the first place? What was the purpose? What was I supposed to learn from the experience? When am I going to finally get over her? I began retreating back to the way I felt when Yasmeen first told me she accepted that job. During the summer we did keep in contact a few times via email. She stated that the job was difficult and she was working six days a week. Even tougher for her was the start of Ramadan and she had fallen ill during that time. While I still did care about Yasmeen, I attempted to separate my feelings for her and not act too concerned with whatever difficulties she was experiencing.

Moreover, I did not take the 'I-told-you-so' attitude because that would just further push her away. I still hoped that eventually she would find her way back to the United States and we could reignite the passion we started in spring.

Labor Day weekend was approaching, school was about to start, and a whole summer wasted drowning myself in self-pity. The self-pity became very comfortable as I avoided getting hurt by not taking any risks meeting new people. Sure, I thought about the axiom 'no risk, no reward'. But my screwed up mind believed that 'no hurt' was the best reward.

I made my way up to Gitana on Labor Day Sunday for my normal Sunday chat, dinner and hookah with Kori. The chat that late afternoon was far from normal.

"So how are you?" asked Kori.

"I'm doing ok, just getting ready for school to start", I replied.

"Have you heard from you know....Yasmeen?"

"Not in a week, I'm sure she's busy".

"Good, the less you contact her, the better for you," Kori said emphatically.

"I guess it would..." I replied but then Kori interrupted me.

"Don't guess...leave her alone and move on," Kori stated with even more emphasis. "You've wasted a whole summer over here wondering about some whore who's not coming back. You should move on already and start talking to new people."

I had always suspected Kori wasn't into Yasmeen especially some of the faces she would make when Yasmeen would ask for extra mint and lemons for her water, but she never had expressed herself to me like that. I appreciated Kori's honesty, albeit a little uncomfortable, however, it's healthy to step out of your comfort zone. For me the comfort zone was the self-pity so any forward progress was better.

"I figured you didn't like her, but what are you trying to tell me?"

"You act like TOO NICE of a guy. You need to get some edge in you," Kori suggested.

I wasn't sure what Kori meant. She had to wait on other customers so I had a chance to reflect on what she said. What did she mean about being 'too nice'? I thought that's how I was supposed to act, considerate and kind, not some arrogant jerk that takes advantage of women.

"What did you mean about a nice guy?" I inquired because this inquiring mind sure wanted to know. Kori's brutal honesty was welcomed but it sure stung.

"Look at you. Yes, I like when you visit, we hang and talk, but you haven't once tried to meet someone else. You won't forget about Yasmeen if you're not distracted."

"Yes I know that but..." as Kori again interrupted me for my lack luster commentary.

"No buts. You sit here closed off to the world reading your magazines, hoping someone would want to meet you. Instead, you're the man you need to take action. The faster you meet someone else, the faster you let go of Yasmeen, the better you will feel about yourself."

What she said made perfect sense, although I was uncomfortable hearing it. I was being destructive to myself by not taking matters into my own hands.

"Kori, that's great and all, but how do I go about it? As you know, I'm not the most confident person right now, I wouldn't even know what to say."

"That doesn't matter. You need to stand up for yourself because right now you come off way too needy and that is UNATTRACTIVE!" Kori insisted.

OUCH! Who gave Kori boxing gloves today? First she threw a left, then a right upper cut. I always follow the tenet 'do what the hot girl says', so I took mental notes. "Ok, but what about this 'nice guy' thing you mentioned? I'm too nice?" I asked.

"Yeah that thing with Yasmeen, calling her and emailing her all the time while she was in Jordan, not good. When you did that, you came off as too needy and not giving her space." Kori stated.

I thought I was being the good 'boyfriend' by trying to stay in contact with her while she was away, although technically we were...well whatever...

"And," Kori continued, "you *will not* give off these nice guy vibes when you start meeting women. You will start going out immediately, stop wasting time and Yasmeen will be out of your mind."

She had such a determined look on her face I leaned back in my chair, held onto the table and opened my eyes really wide. I had never heard this from her before but *DAMN*, what a reality check. I'll follow what the hot girl says. It was an eye-opening conversation and over the course of the next two weeks, we called each other or contacted via email. This friendship was now growing steadily and I certainly appreciated it. Although Kori is HOT herself, becoming friends with her was entirely *more important* to me than if I tried to "talk" to her. I would not be attracted to her in *that* way.

Football season had started so I was going out again with friends to watch the games and have a good time. As a result, I experienced happier times rather than staying home alone. I subsequently moved into a better apartment, so I was definitely feeling elevated about myself. I hadn't contacted Yasmeen in a while and even though I felt that urge, I kept in mind what Kori suggested. Actually, it had been a while since

I saw Kori too, so I ventured up to Gitana for a visit.

"Hey stranger, where have you been?" Kori stated excitedly as we hugged.

"Been trying to keep busy as you suggested, oh wise one."

"Have you talked to Yasmeen?"

"No." I quickly replied.

"Good. Now what about meeting others?"

"I haven't... had the...I haven't tried," I stuttered. Although I had been going out, I wasn't confident yet to approach anyone. I actually tried my hand at online dating but out of the 25 email messages I sent out, I had exactly one response. So I guess I gave off the 'nice guy' vibes over the computer as well.

"You have to behave almost like a bad boy type now, more edgy. That's much more attractive. Leave Mr. Nice Guy at home," suggested Kori.

I told Kori that I had heard about bad boys before, but I figured these were the guys on motorcycles with tons of tattoos, loud and obnoxious behavior. I had been married for 14 years, had I been out of the dating game that long? Had things changed that much? If I needed to get the proverbial midlife crisis things like tattoos, motorcycle, and dye my hair (my head is shaved) then maybe becoming a monk would be advantageous.

"What I mean is that you have to approach a woman with confidence, without a care in the world, even if you internally don't feel it, you have to start doing so and eventually it will come naturally. Don't put us on a pedestal, we feel just as insecure as you do. Don't call us everyday, make us miss you." Kori suggested.

"So this is not about being loud, obnoxious and abusive then. I had always heard women were attracted to bad boys types." I stated inquisitively.

"This is more about being *edgy*. If you give a woman all

of your attention, what more could she ask for? Then you become boring and not a challenge. Women like challenges. Hold back a little bit, don't call back or text right away. If a woman doesn't know whether you like her or not immediately, that's great. Try it." Kori recommended.

So now for the second time this year another woman much younger than me is teaching me something. Wow, how I like learning from younger women!

A few nights later I went to a bar I had frequented for a long time. As had been the custom during the summer, I went by myself and became friendly with a couple of the servers. They, of course, were amicable because it leads to better tips! I noticed a group of people, six men and three women, whom seemed as though they knew each other from work. I looked over at one of the women and she happened to stare back. I still felt timid but I glanced at her several times and she back at me. The group wanted to take a picture and so I quickly volunteered to take it for them. I figured that could be my 'in'. Two people from the group were married the rest were just work friends. Turns out that the leader of the group was running for mayor of Santa Ana. I decided I would talk a bit to him *before* I made my move on the girl I was eyeing. After talking with him for a while, I turned to her and included her into our conversation. After a while, I talked only to her and we chatted and flirted nearly an hour. People in the group started to leave so I became nervous about asking her for her phone number. Just as I turned I felt her hand grab my thigh, it was a piece of paper with her name and number on it. Wow! I couldn't believe a whole summer wasted isolating myself in pity and anger. I was so excited I texted Kori that night. It may seem childish, but I had felt so down about myself for nearly four months that any good news was certainly welcomed. Kori called right back and inquired how the night went down.

"I followed your advice, didn't talk too much about myself, kept the conversation going with humor and interesting stories...your recipe worked." I gloated.

"Wow, I'm so proud of you, but don't stop there. Talk to as many women as possible, get many numbers because you want to be the selector. Be the man." Kori insisted.

Sometimes all we need is to create some small victories to give ourselves more confidence to have even greater success with future interactions. This is not necessarily in relationships with women, but also with your family, your coworkers, or your boss, whatever. Incremental steps help you escape the despair you feel.

Later the same week, I was on a field trip with school AND I began talking to one of the chaperones on the trip. She turned out to be the aunt of one my students. OOPS, that's tricky. Kori's words stayed in my mind so after the bus dropped everyone off, I found myself with another number and a date. Wow, I was shocked and my confidence started to come back. I also received an email from one of the contacts I made online. Another response! So my next trip up to Gitana, I actually had some more good news to report to Kori.

"Hey you, you look a little different," Kori stated.

"I feel different! I now have 2 more dates coming up," I confidently told Kori.

"Playa!" she exclaimed.

"One I met on a field trip and the other was from online. One lives not too far from me and the other lives not too far from this restaurant." I informed her.

"Bring them if you can, let me meet them." Kori stated emphatically.

So I did that. I took Kori's advice and my confidence increased tremendously, now sky high. I met the online girl at Gitana one night and the next night I brought the aunt of one of my students. Both dates went quite well and there were future dates planned. Now time to debrief with Kori the next time I visited her.

"I think they are both cool, so what do you think?" I inquired.

"This is a good start." Kori interjected. "I think they will be ok for now, but you will meet even better women very soon. You have changed, you LOOK more confident and that comes off as much more attractive."

"You are right Kori, I FEEL more confidence now and that must translate into how I talk to people, not just women but in my interactions with others." I informed her.

"See, you take matters into your own hands instead of waiting around letting others make decisions for you. The YOU from the summer is going away. So have you heard from Yasmeen?" Kori asked.

"I talked with her briefly the other day, I guess I still have feelings for her, but talking to others is making me finally feel better about myself." I said.

"Keep it up and you will soon be saying, Yasmeen who?"

We both laughed at that, but she, as usual, was right on. Even though I still had feelings for Yasmeen, she was FAR away and that helped me concentrate on making myself feel better about ME. Yes, I made myself suffer when Yasmeen left, I couldn't blame Yasmeen for how I felt; it was a choice I made whether I wanted to see it or not. Kori helped me understand that and the confidence I was now feeling was another *choice* I had made. Was that the reason for meeting Yasmeen in the first place? Who knows, it's hard to evaluate all of the circumstances in our life, however, the defeated man refuses to learn from his mistakes. It's the better man that learns from his experiences and works to change the circumstances of those mistakes to avoid similar failures in the future. Over the course of the next few months I introduced Kori to a number of other women, and she always gave me her honest opinions. What a tremendous blessing to have Kori as a friend, she helped me see the light, the light within myself that I had put out for months.

5

Reflection

AS A MIDDLE-AGED, divorced man, I had preconceptions and misconceptions about how others would perceive me and what my course of action would be for my future. I had to start over now and I carried with me so many limiting self-beliefs. I figured I was 'damaged-goods' and would come across that way to others. I am divorced, in my early 40s, have children, and drive a van. Sure as a teacher, that would be considered a good job, but certainly not one that would have the ladies lining up to meet me. Teacher and ladies are usually not in the same sentence. I also believed that women were interested only in good-looking guys and I perceive myself to be a 'very average' looking guy. I didn't think I would have a solid chance to meet people. Moreover, after divorcing and settling costs, childcare and child support, that usually didn't leave me much money at the end of the month either. So it was an uphill struggle for me with all of this 'baggage'.

With so many negatives coming out of a marriage, I usually kept to myself until I met Yasmeen. She didn't care about any of those insecurities and negativities that I had and this is what made the relationship special at that time.

She overlooked all of that and concentrated on my positives. Even at times when money was short and she wanted to see me, she generously paid for our dates until I was able to contribute again. We both gave to the relationship back and forth and that aspect made it so tough to have the relationship end when it did. I was feeling extremely good about myself. When she stayed in Jordan, this led to my downward spiraling lack of confidence. Admittedly, the relationship I entered with Yasmeen would be categorized as a rebound relationship, for both of us. I had not really taken the time to heal from my divorce before I met her. Nor had I developed a strategy for starting over. There was obviously nothing I could do, the attraction for Yasmeen was real as soon as we first met and we talked as though we had always known each other. She admitted to feeling the same way about me.

Then Yasmeen left, I decided to withdraw myself and build a wall around me, instead of taking the time to recover. Building walls does not help the healing process rather it only extends the suffering.

I recall looking at my father after his divorce from my mother. It has been 20 years since that time and I can tell he still hasn't healed. He decided to become a recluse and build walls around him. That is not how I wanted to live my life, but I started doing just that after Yasmeen left. Am I glad I made the decision to turn my life around and stand up for myself. It was ironic that I rented the same cheap apartment that my father did. I know that he feared rejection and I definitely became fearful of falling into his same trap.

Just like the divorced man, a woman similarly may have experienced a divorce or break up so she will want something different at that point as well. Timing can be everything and a man may meet a woman at the wrong time. This probably was my experience with Yasmeen, she seemed like the right woman, but it was the wrong time, so it couldn't work. When a man is starting over, he may initially experience some rejection as I did many times. Understand that rejection will happen mostly for reasons that are beyond our control, such as:

a. Foul mood ('I don't wanna be here') – if a woman is not in a good mood, it's a choice that she has made, so move on to someone that is ready to meet someone new and have fun. When you are feeling happy and confident about yourself, you don't want anyone dragging you down.

b. Negativity - ('men are pigs') – no matter how hot a woman appears, a man does not want to meet a negative woman whom will bring him down. You will be able to tell by her negative body language, facial expressions and the vocabulary that she uses reflects 'the glass is half empty'.

c. Recent break-up ('woe is me') – someone who has been recently hurt will not be ready to meet someone new. This woman could be in the healing process too and perhaps is out only to converse with her friends to get over her ex-boyfriend or ex-husband. She will still have strong feelings for the ex, and if you try to meet her, you too may be devastated if she runs back to the ex.

d. Rejecting your advance – a woman may have certain wants or needs at a particular time. Since it is this aspect of rejection that we control, this will be developed in the next chapter.

Sometimes you may happen to surpass all of these negative aspects and a woman may agree to give you her number or even to a date, only to flake out on you later. As a man, don't get down about yourself or even react to her; this is a negative reflection of the woman. It demonstrates her dishonesty and lack of confidence in *herself* to give you a true answer about her feelings toward you. It's easier for her to text you and flake rather than call you on the phone or tell you face-to-face. I would rather a woman deny me immediately so I don't waste my time and effort and be strung along with possibilities. Expect a certain percentage of flakes when meeting women, and always have a back-up plan. Life does happen, and things truly do come up. As a divorced man, you have to anticipate that she may have situations come up with her job, or more likely with her children. If a woman is seriously interested in rescheduling a date, carefully but FIRMLY inform her how valuable *your* time is and that you appreciate 100% confirmation this time. This shows that you have self-esteem and command respect from her. I had to deal with similar situations and to reassure myself that a woman who behaves this way is not worthy of my time. Remember, a woman that is TRULY interested in you WILL NOT flake.

After life experiences, it is important to reflect on the mistakes and the successes one has. It is easiest to blame others for causing us to feel a certain way. I opine that what we feel, for the most part, is the effect of *choices we make;* a response to certain stimuli or chain of events. We naturally feel pain due to loss, but the amount of suffering we experience is a choice. When Yasmeen originally left for Jordan, I could have selected a number of paths including dating others, or wait to see what happens when (or if) she returned. Similarly I had to balance the options *she* had and consider seriously the distinct possibility that Yasmeen would not return. I chose, however, to wait it out and see what happens. Since I took the 'see-what-happens' stance, I should have prepared myself for the alternative that she would stay in Jordan forever. I didn't do that. So in reality, the anger I immediately felt should have been turned inward for my decision to wait it out. Later, when she confirmed that she had found a job and not returning, once again I was confronted with a number of decisions to make. To my detriment, I chose to withdraw myself due to the hurt I felt knowing that she was not coming back to me. Although the pain of separation will naturally last for a while, the depth of the suffering resulted from *decisions I made* and not something I was unable to control.

We tend to make excuses as a 'cop out' to make ourselves feel better. Certainly, when things don't develop the way we planned or hoped for, we feel sadness, anger and hurt. How we respond after a set of circumstances that occur in our lives is completely *our own*. People may drown their sorrows with extreme behavior such as overeating, over spending, abusing alcohol or drugs etc. In retrospect, I should have taken control of my feelings and actions to make the situation after Yasmeen better for me. I didn't do that, so I suffered months of hurt and anguish as a result of *my* actions and not anyone else's.

Unfortunately, time passes and one can *never* replace the lost time. People waste time and lament over situations they cannot influence instead of empowering themselves in areas under their management. *We ultimately cannot control the motivations and decisions of others.* With better knowledge now, I have moved forward and in the future I will not make the same mistakes again (well, at least try not to).

One decision that benefited me tremendously was to have Kori as a friend and confidante. Some 'pick-up artists' suggest not becoming friends with women you meet. However, from my experience, I discovered a treasure in having Kori by my side. She is not related to or friends with anyone around me. Hence, she offered me honest and unbiased feedback on how my behavior was detrimental to me. Sometimes her feedback was direct and painful, but it was a welcomed 'wake-up' call to circumstances around me. Furthermore, developing our friendship and listening to her perspective on relationships helped me gain the confidence that I desired to make myself a better man.

Becoming the better man is a lifelong endeavor. President John F. Kennedy in his speech at Rice University, September 12, 1962, regarding the race to the moon said:

"We choose to go to the moon in this decade and do the other things, not because they are easy but because *they are hard*. Because that goal will serve to organize the best of our energies and skills because that challenge is one we are willing to accept, one we are unwilling to postpone and one we intend to win."

Bouncing back from tough situations is difficult but it is a challenge the better man accepts readily and does not postpone. He meets it head on. A man will not be victorious in every life circumstance but the better man learns to twist that defeat into a victory later in life (sometimes even the next night). This was a life lesson for me as I wallowed in self-pity for a whole summer.

6

Becoming a Better Man

A DIVORCE OR separation is not the final verdict on the value of a man. Likewise, losing a job or getting fired is not either. Rather, our response to tough situations is the superior litmus test of a man's worth. It serves as a fresh opportunity to enhance our lives since what we feel about ourselves is more important than what others think. It is this quest to restore our own masculinity that keeps us alive.

A man must continuously improve himself to increase his self-worth and this translates more positively on how others perceive us. The questions, misconceptions and insecurities a man deals with after divorcing or separating are natural but not impossible to overcome. These insecurities we feel will manifest intermittently and we must handle them as they come. It is imperative to develop a strategy for making oneself a better man in dealing with the assortment of relationships in our lives, not just with women, but also our families, children, career etc. The important variable following a divorce or separation is to allow enough time to restore a man's confidence and develop a strategy for beginning anew.

How can a man accomplish this successfully? The following are some things I have learned through trial and error (lots of errors), research and interviews with scores of women.

One question men have longed to find the direct answer to is 'what does a woman want?' There was even a movie about this question, yet was there a definitive answer? All jokes aside, of the research and interviews, women tend to agree the number one factor in peaking a woman's interest in a man is confidence. A confident man tends to put a woman at ease and makes her more likely to invest some time in getting to know him. A woman desires to feel like a woman, not a mom, nag or therapist when she is with you. The confident man will attract quality women.

Let's start with some overly general definitions so we can understand the categories of men, given that there exists some gradients between each type.

- The **'nice guy'** is the one that will bend over backwards for the woman, always call, and always be there whenever a woman needs him. While ultimately this is the type of behavior that a woman desires in a man, this is not the behavior that tends to initially attract a woman. The nice guy invariably displays more supplicating behavior rather than confident one. He is quite predictable, overly romantic and gives his all to the woman upon meeting her. This may repulse a woman and she will likely consider this type of behavior creepy.
- The **'bad boy'** or **'jerk'** displays extreme confidence and independence, which is attractive to a woman in the beginning. First, the 'bad boy' doesn't let anyone take advantage of him and remains self-centered. Second, the 'bad boy' is spontaneous and fun, constantly changing ideas, meeting places and handling

himself differently than other men. This throws a woman off and this aspect is distinguishable from the normal predictable nice guy. Third, the 'bad boy' is so independent he is not interested in kissing anyone's butt and seeking approval from anyone. The bad boy attracts a woman at a strong, emotional level. His behavior, however, is the one that later tends to be too controlling and abusive to women physically and emotionally. As a result, the relationship leads to volatility and expends negative time and energy for both parties.

- The **edgy guy** also exhibits much confidence in himself and elicits aloof behavior. This is a terrific hook to a female since she may not be cognizant of whether this man has genuine interest in her or not. The edgy guy is the balance between a controlling jerk and the supplicating nice guy. This man does not rely on a woman for his overall happiness. He is complete within himself and seeks a woman to share his confidence and successful attitude. He can easily make his own decisions and is quite comfortable in doing so which again leads to attraction.

The belief that women are attracted to bad boys and jerks has some truth to it. In the attraction continuum, bad boys and jerks tend to present themselves with confidence and that is the number one attraction for women. Thus, initially these bad boys and jerks exhibit the type of behavior a woman finds attractive. They exude self-assurance, are comfortable with their own being, go after what they want and *respect themselves*. It is not until later on in the relationship that the bad boy reveals his true colors. By then a woman is hooked on the challenge of possibly changing him from the jerk/bad boy into the nice guy behaviors that she really desires. She may even sacrifice her own needs to do so. This situation is not one for the better man (edgy guy) to live with.

ATTRACTION CHARACTERISTICS

I ASKED THE question earlier 'what does a woman want'? A woman desires distinct qualities from a man at various times in her life. A woman will want something different upon the first meeting with a man than what she will want on a third date or the first year anniversary. Before we contemplate the future, let's develop a discussion for first meeting a woman. Erase from your mind all of the advice you see on TV and the movies, it does not work in the real world the overwhelming majority of the time.

There are certain characteristics that will open a woman's curiosity in a man. We mentioned confidence is the number one feature of attraction. Other attractive personality traits include:

a. <u>Fun/Spontaneity</u> – a woman wants to hang out with somebody that exudes energy and positive feelings in her. A woman aroused on an emotional level will more likely feel attracted to you. The better man behaves conspicuously different from the average man out there and looks for ways to stimulate this energy within her. Plan exciting events other than the usual (and boring) dinner and movie.

b. <u>Clean, polished appearance</u> – a woman is more concerned with a man's clean appearance rather than if a man is good-looking or not. Actually, some women turn off to overly handsome guys because they will judge him a 'player'. A good-looking man does have a perceived advantage at first, however, this is temporary.

Perhaps you may have put on a few pounds during the marriage, lose them now. Part of regaining confidence is looking good and feeling good. Wearing clothes that actually match, wearing clothes that are pressed, and wearing clean shoes etc, are more important factors. Make your tailor your best friend, don't just buy pants from a discount store, have the pants tapered as well for a better fit. Don't wear clothes that are obviously well below your age. You will come across as a nerd or trying too hard; celebrate the age you are at. NEVER WEAR SNEAKERS (unless you are exercising) OR FLIP-FLOPS (unless you are at the beach). Clean, polished shoes make you most presentable. Since women have a better sense of smell than men, fresh breath and great cologne are indispensable.

c. Masterfully Conversant – quality women will be more attracted to a man that can hold an intelligent conversation rather than someone who stumbles when he talks or is not knowledgeable in common subjects. A routine joke among my female friends goes like this: "I was definitely attracted to him... until he opened his mouth." DO YOUR HOMEWORK before going out. Brush up on current events, trends, movies, music, etc. Check out what going on in the community during the coming days. There may be an event a woman is interested in attending and if you already know about it, that puts you ahead of the average guy. **Knowledge** is power and makes you more interesting to meet. Another essential part of conversation is LISTENING. Allow the woman to do most of the talking and interject at different times without giving advice or spouting out statistics. When you do chime in, challenge something she says in a positive way not abrasively. This rapport you develop demonstrates that you are not afraid to offer your opinion that differs from hers. This leads to even greater conversation and shows that you have cognitions and ideas that are to be respected, unlike the supplicating 'nice guy'. Women will constantly test your manhood and this never ends even once you start dating or marry a woman. However, try not to let a woman's test deflate your ego, *instead she wants to feel the power of your masculinity*. A woman despises a weak man whom will just agree with everything a woman says and allows her to lead conversation. A quality woman welcomes a challenge. You can demonstrate listening skills and controlling the conversation skills by using words such as "go on", "describe that" or "how did that make you feel?" Funny stories, adventures and mishaps are all topics that keep the conversation light as you become more interesting to talk to. Stay clear, however, of topics such as religion, politics, exes and especially sex. Upon first meeting someone, you don't want to give off the impression that sex is the only reason you are talking to her. That may turn her off immediately and you have eliminated yourself from possibly meeting a fantastic woman.

The basic traits of confidence, spontaneity, clean appearance, and great conversation help you look more attractive to a woman. These are aspects of our personality that we can control and develop. When we put our best foot forward and avoid common mistakes, the likelihood of success in meeting others increases dramatically. The last characteristic of rejection we mentioned in the previous chapter was "rejecting your advance". Unfortunately, one mistake may eliminate us from meeting the woman we want. That may seem unfair since most men are more forgiving of women when they make mistakes (that is usually because we are interested in getting in their skirts).

There are other traits that we will discuss throughout the rest of the book. The better man leaves his comfort zone and learns something culturally new such as dance, language, art, music etc. You never know whom you may meet throughout your life since there are more than 3.5 billion women from myriads of cultures around the world. Don't eliminate the best women of the world just because you are not knowledgeable with a new language or culture; think outside the box. Trying new things can be the best decision for you, something absolutely different from what you have experienced before. An enormous advantage about residing in the United States is that women from all parts of the globe live here. Moreover, in my experience I have found that women of a different culture appreciate a man whom is willing to take that risk and try something new. The better man is a lifelong learner. Again, let's take another quote this time from world famous boxer Muhammad Ali: "If you believe at 50 what you believed at 20, then you have wasted 30 years." Your circumstances will not improve unless you make a concerted effort to educate and acquire different skills than you did in the past.

The unconfident man believes quality women are in short supply, known as the 'scarcity principle'. Notice the root word is 'scarce.' To the better, confident man the world is abundantly full of quality woman. Let's use an example from baseball. A batter that has been in a hitting slump sees marbles as the pitcher throws the next pitch; he is unconfident and thinking too much about his struggles. A batter that is in the middle of a hitting streak sees nothing but beach balls thrown at him and is always ready to smack the ball out of the stadium because his confidence is sky high. Exude the confidence of hitting beach balls when meeting women.

Some of the best situations for the divorced man to meet others would be through friends, or at parties, at coffee shops, with meeting groups, etc. Avoid the club scene, it is probably a scene best left for the immature. Lounges and bars are other places to meet people.

In order to better comprehend how to become the better man, let's study some traits that men need to avoid altogether in meeting situations.

NEGATIVE BODY LANGUAGE

THE OVERWHELMING PERCENTAGE of communication is through body language. Typically, women are more adept than the most men when it comes to noticing body language. Women are similar to football coaches. The football coach will peer at a player and judge how he conducts himself on the field through his body language and what his eyes reveal. The coach can read whether that player is ready to catch the game-winning touchdown pass or if he should call on another player for that key play. When it's time to meet people, you want the coach to call your number. Let's review some key body language mistakes that the better man avoids.

    a. <u>Posture</u> – the unconfident man will stand too uptight and rigid or have rolled, slumped over shoulders appearing as though he doesn't want to be noticed or take up too much space. Or when sitting down, he is slumping over his drink or his food. This immediately signals to a female this guy lacks any kind of confidence, is not fun to be around right now and just wants to be by himself. A woman would gladly stroll on by to the next more confident gentleman.

The better man stands upright naturally, relaxed, with a confident smile. While standing, he will lean comfortably against a wall or post. If seated, he will sit upright, with open posture.

b. Facial expressions – there is no better facial expression than the smile. Use an inviting natural smile frequently to convey the confidence you feel on the inside. The unconfident man will show a facially listless or gloomy expression and women can read that a mile a way. If you are ready to look at or approach a woman do so with a smile, it's an invitation to someone that is confident and exciting.

c. Hands – the position of the hands also gives off signals. The unconfident man will fidget with the hands nervously by fiddling with things like his drink or constantly touching his face. NEVER PUT YOUR HANDS IN YOUR POCKETS NOR HAVE ARMS FOLDED IN FRONT OF YOU. This displays a closed-off appearance as though you are not ready to interact with anyone. The confident man will keep the hands away from the face and pockets and stands with open body language arms to his side. If necessary, place a finger through a belt loop to show a relaxed appearance. When talking, the confident man gesticulates naturally to display interest in his conversation.

d. Eye contact – the unconfident man will constantly look around the room nervously. He will stare at a woman and that consequently makes her feel uncomfortable; she will regard him as creepy. When talking, he will constantly look down or away. This signals to the female that this man is either not confident in what he is saying or is being untruthful. The better man makes constant eye contact with the person he is talking to. His eyes do not dart around the room nervously rather he looks in a particular direction for a few seconds then slowly looks elsewhere. When he spies a female he will make eye contact for no more than three seconds and then smile. Again this exhibits self-assured behavior and will more likely peak interest in him.

By avoiding some of these common mistakes, the better man enhances his chances of meeting someone. A powerful exhibition of a confident man projecting true masculinity demonstrates higher value and leads to attraction in others.

Now we turn our attention to the first meeting. While we may be confident and project ourselves as such, there will still exist some anxiety when approaching someone for the first time. The divorced man may not have tried to meet someone for a long time, so nervousness is natural but that doesn't mean we need to tip the female off to our apprehension.

THE APPROACH

LET'S SAY YOU are at a friend's party. Just about everyone in attendance is a friend of a friend, someone at the party knows someone else. Approaching in that environment can be more comfortable because there is at least one topic of conversation in common – the person whom you may know that's throwing the party. Plus you are already spoken for because you know other people there, you are not as much of a stranger. At the bar or lounge approaching may be more uncomfortable because you have to approach as a stranger. However, if you mess it up, there are other fish in the sea and people there don't know each other. Each situation has its advantages and disadvantages. We listed in the previous chapter the reasons for rejection and 75% of the time it has nothing to do with the man. Either way you can develop a strategy for minimizing the chances of rejection. Even if a woman is not interested in meeting you, the overwhelming majority of the time, it is not about you.

Let's say you are out with your friends and you notice an interesting woman across the room. First thing try to make eye contact, hold for three seconds and smile. You are trying to get a reaction from the female to see if she may be receptive to an approach. Try this a few times to see if you get any reaction. This lessens the chance of you wasting your time walking over to her trying to talk to someone that is not interested in you. If you do receive a smile and some eye contact than this is an invitation for you to attempt to make a connection.

So you make your way across the room, what do you say?

It is this aspect right here that is keeping you in your seat or leaning against the wall all night, not knowing what to say. I struggled with this aspect so much of not knowing how to begin an interaction. That's why earlier I suggested DO YOUR HOMEWORK. Kori challenged me by saying "you're the man". Humor is also a great way to introduce yourself as a fun, innovative type of man. In the first chapter I described how I played on Yasmeen's words as she introduced herself, "Hi, I'm Early" to which I replied "Hello, Early, I'm Luis". I took a risk at humor and it worked (very well).

There are a myriad of ways to open conversation with a female. You can simply introduce yourself, ask her for an opinion, make a comment about the party, bar or lounge you are in, or walk over and give her a compliment. ANYTHING as long as the man is starting the interaction. If you compliment a woman make sure it has nothing to do with her looks. For instance, you may like the shoes she is wearing or she may have interesting accessories. Make a comment about how you like them and that she made a great choice. This places the compliment on something she can control, a decision, not whether she is beautiful or not. Many men worry about their opening lines when meeting women. The opening serves to get the woman's attention to you. What's as important is the follow-up. Yes, now you have her attention what do you say? This is where doing your homework comes into play as well as using encouraging words such as "what do you mean by that?", "how did that make you feel?", or "please tell me more". Again using words such as these allows the woman to open up and give you more insight into her being. Remember, you want the woman to do most of the talking and then interject some of your own thoughts or make a comment on what she just said. This leads to more interesting conversation and *you* can make a decision whether she is interesting enough *for you* or you need to look elsewhere. The MAN is the selector.

Once you have approached with your opening line take a notice of *her* body language. Since we have discussed your confident body language now take a look at hers to see if you are making an impact; you do not want to spend time with someone whom is not interested in you. As we stated earlier a woman is programmed to say no for various reasons, so convince her that you are worth getting to know by your approach and comforting body language. Examples of her body language that tips the scale in your favor include:

a. Moving closer to you during conversation – at a loud club or lounge when engrossed in conversation it may be natural for her to move closer to you to hear you. However, if she stays within that space that may be a good indication of interest.

b. Seeking your attention – a woman may laugh at your jokes (even if they are not funny), exaggerate her gesticulations or facial expressions, play with or flick her hair, etc. Moreover, she may even give you a playful nickname, such as heartbreaker or player, and even make a comment as though you have a girlfriend just to see if you have one. These movements and comments are meant to focus your attention on her for the moment.

c. Demonstrating enthusiasm - she maintains eye contact with you during conversation tuning everything else out and keeps smiling during the interaction. Or if there is a lull in the conversation she may quickly move to a different topic to keep the conversation going. These are positive signs the interaction is progressing well.

d. Touching – in eagerness to subtly display interest, she may playfully push or lightly punch you during conversation, touch you as she is talking, brush up against you or keep a body part leaning against you while talking.

All of these and others similar types of positioning are considered positive signs that she has curiosity in you. With this knowledge it's up to you to keep her interested further.

Opposite body language such as moving further away from you, looking around the room over your shoulder, and keeping her arms folded in front of her gives you an indication that she is NOT interested in you or perhaps keeping you around until someone better comes along. A woman looking over your shoulders may do what's called the 'help me eyes' to a friend or even stranger to take her away from you. So watch her body language as well as taking care of your own. Remember you are displaying total confident body language all the while, and you always assume that she is interested in you. Too many times a man approaches in the hopes the woman will like him; we need to change that belief, the better man wants to be in the position of selector.

7

What the Women Say

WE HAVE BRIEFLY discussed body language and approach; it is impossible to outline what to do in every possible scenario. Of utmost importance is the confidence a man displays when meeting females. Lets see what some of the women I interviewed say about their wants, approaches and turn-offs. I interviewed scores of women and we will discuss some of the results of specific women from different cultural backgrounds. *My comments are italicized.*

Name: Mercedes (in a relationship)
Age: 38
Ethnicity: Mexican

What is your perception of what women want?

A man to love and respect someone emotionally supportive, that can feel love, and be there for them when they need it. A man that is ready to understand and listen and hear what WE are saying. A true love will do that.

- *Notice that this sounds exactly like the nice guy. However.....*

What kinds of guys attract you?

A man that is strong, independent and not too needy. A man that is confident in showing strong feelings and affections for me.

- *Notice in the attraction phase she wants someone strong and independent. More like the edgy guy or bad boy.*

What is the number one thing that turns you off about guys?

Someone who is self-centered and not emotionally connected. Someone who can't control his temper and doesn't listen.

- *This is where your cool, confident demeanor comes in. This is the opposite of the bad boy/jerk.*

What is the number one mistake a man makes when approaching women?

A guy that comes off too strong and talks about how beautiful and sexy I am. Someone who shows off how much money he has.

- *So notice here again, take it easy with the comments on her physical looks and sex. If you have money, it is a turnoff to brag. Take a look at the answer to question #5.*

What can men do that would make you more attracted to them?

I become more attracted if a man does not cross any sexual boundaries when first talking to me. It shows respect.

Name: Ka (married)
Age: 29
Ethnicity: Asian/Buddhist

What is your perception of what women want?

A challenge. For me to figure out what the man wants.

- *Here she perceives interest in someone that she has to work for. If you simply agree with what she says, she will move on.*

What kinds of guys attract you?

I like Hispanic guys and someone who is humble.

- *Here she likes someone of different cultural background and someone who presents himself in a quiet, confident manner.*

What is the number one thing that turns you off about guys?

Cockiness – bragging about self. This shows they are experts in that area only and not worldly.

- *Remember that knowledge is power.*

What is the number one mistake a man makes when approaching women?

Too confident that they think they will get your number.

- *Approach a woman with modest confidence that she already likes you and not 'hoping' that she will.*

What can men do that would make you more attracted to them?

Play hard to get and that he is not easily achievable.

- *A quality woman likes a challenge. If she can have you already, the challenge is over.*

Name: Liz (engaged)
Age: 25
Ethnicity: White/Jewish

What is your perception of what women want?

The majority of women want short cuts – finding a sugar daddy and a lot are clingy – need your attention all the time.

These women want money, house in suburbs, compete with Joneses, nice cars with as little effort from them as possible. Even though woman have fought for equality, they are still stuck in 1950s model, women at home, man at work, giving money to them.

- *This was probably the most honest answer of all the interviews done. While I'll admit some women you run into will want this, you can eliminate them based on the conversation, as they will portray themselves as too materialistic (gold digger). A woman that likes you for you is a better choice.*

What kinds of guys attract you?

Intelligent, eclectic, urbane, sense of humor, easy going, mysterious, someone that has an "I don't care attitude." Look at a man's hands, tells a lot about a person.

- *We mentioned before knowledge is power. A man that gives off a fun attitude is more attractive. Plus we discussed the message your hands give off.*

What is the number one thing that turns you off about guys?

Someone who is arrogant, flashing money (talking about it), smugness and conceitedness, having no beliefs of his own, one that follows the crowd, someone not sure of himself, has poor vocabulary and can't laugh at himself.

- *So this is more than one thing, but it is part and parcel to what we have discussed herein.*

What is the number one mistake a man makes when approaching women?

Having low eye contact (to breasts), and approaching me with smugness and overconfidence.

- *Maintain eye contact (to her eyes) and keep your attention to her and not her body parts. This makes her feel like a woman and not an object.*

What can men do that would make you more attracted to them?

Start an intelligent conversation, being humorous with funny sarcastic remarks (not directed towards me), and display confidence and sincerity in who they are.

- *Knowledge and confidence is power.*

Name: Cindy (single)
Age: 45
Ethnicity: Mexican

What is your perception of what women want?

A woman wants affection, attention (loving and sexual) as though you are the only woman in the world to them. Also a woman wants faithfulness, gentleness, and kindness.

What kinds of guys attract you?

A man that is brash and abrasive with the Bad Boy Type of look. I like the challenge of taming the bad boy.

- *Compare the answer to the first question with the answer to the second. What attracts her is a confident man, someone who is dripping with masculinity. Then her goal is to tame him to what she really wants. However, the better man is not 'tamed', maintain your masculinity and her attraction continues.*

What is the number one thing that turns you off about guys?

A guy with wandering eyes who is talking about other women while with me.

- *Keep you attention to the woman you're talking to at the time.*

What is the number one mistake a man makes when approaching women?

Trying to be too forceful and try to use vulnerabilities against you.

- *Women want you to convince them that you are a good catch. They do not want to be made to feel lower than you in order to be attracted to you. It is repulsive to them.*

What can men do that would make you more attracted to them?

Be persistent in a nice way.

- *Not in a creepy, stalker type of way.*

Name: Ruth (married 14 years)
Age: 32
Ethnicity: Mexican

What is your perception of what women want?

Good-looking guy who is compassionate, thoughtful, caring for a persons feelings, considerate and loving.

- *Again this is her perception of what a woman wants. This goes right to the stereotype that woman want a good-looking guy. While looks do attract, it is more the personality that will keep a man around. Read answer #2.*

What kinds of guys attract you?

A man who is hard-working, good listener, educated, good looking, grungy-type, loving, understanding and taking care of family.

- *Notice the qualities.*

What is the number one thing that turns you off about guys?

A guy that's too into himself – always looking in the mirror, too picky about things and trying too hard. The momma's boy complex kills any attraction.

- *If you are too into yourself, you exclude her because ultimately she desires inclusion. A supplicating man (momma's boy) is eliminated.*

What is the number one mistake a man makes when approaching women?

Giving me a dumb pick up line and trying too hard to talk to me. Always hanging around me.

- *NO PICK UP LINES. Those are for amateurs and those that are not confident. If you try too hard (like stalking), that turns off a woman. Balance is key.*

What can men do that would make you more attracted to them?

Be a good communicator. More compassionate, honest and sincere.

- *This goes back to your confident approach.*

Name: Wendy (in a relationship)
Age: 41
Ethnicity: Venezuelan

What is your perception of what women want?

It depends on age and maturity. Younger women want money, a career, and to find themselves. Older women are more interested in stability and trust then worry about security (money).

- *Here she separated wants based on age, which as we mentioned before, women's wants change over time. So be cognizant of the type or age of the woman you approach. As an older, divorced man don't eliminate a younger woman because of your age, it can be quite exciting to date a younger woman and make you feel younger too.*

What kinds of guys attract you?

I am attracted to white guys, tall, with a career and someone who is settled down, with a "family frame of mind".

- *As a seasoned female, she does not want to 'chase' younger guys, she desires someone who is settled. She is also attracted to someone outside of her own culture.*

What is the number one thing that turns you off about guys?

Someone that is needy, jealous, demanding and possessive.

- *This is why you keep a self-assured aura around you. The above descriptions are not.*

What is the number one mistake a man makes when approaching women?

They only have sex in mind.

- *Eventually sex is a great experience, however, a woman does not want to feel that is the only thing on your mind. You want to create sexual tension; that is different than wanting sex. You want her to perceive that sex is her idea and that she is in control of that response. Your self-assured demeanor, playful teasing and appropriate touching may convince her it's a good idea.*

What can men do that would make you more attracted to them?

Be fun, honest and respectful.

- *A relaxed, fun atmosphere will create attraction*

Name: Melody (single)
Age: 25
Ethnicity: African American

What is your perception of what women want?

A woman wants faithfulness, stability, and love.

What kinds of guys attract you?

Black or Hispanic guys, some white guys that are with rocker, preppy or GQ look, even some with hip hop style.

- *This girl initially is attracted to a number of different types and styles. The better man creates his own style of attractiveness and does not try to copy others. Again, she seems to have attraction for others outside of her ethnic group.*

What is the number one thing that turns you off about guys?

A man that wears dirty, old white shoes and bad breath.

- *This goes back to clean, fresh appearance and smell. Never wear sneakers.*

What is the number one mistake a man makes when approaching women?

A man trying to use cheesy ass pick-up lines and being too grabby.

- *The better man approaches with fresh, original topics of conversation. Only appropriate type of touching that is natural during conversation.*

What can men do that would make you more attracted to them?

An honest man that considers other's feelings without being too blunt.

- *If you can't consider another's feelings, she will feel that you won't consider her feelings as important.*

Name: Darlene (single)
Age: 23
Ethnicity: White

What is your perception of what women want?

A woman wants a man who is faithful, who has a good job, loves kids and the ability to love her.

What kinds of guys attract you?

A clean-cut, educated man who has a solid career. A man who is older and stable.

- *She as a 20-something is interested in a man older than she is.*

What is the number one thing that turns you off about guys?

Someone who has a sloppy appearance, smells like work and has dirty fingernails.

- *Here for the second time she mentions a clean-cut appearance. In follow-up questions, she stated this was more important to her than if a guy is good-looking. She admitted she may look twice at a good-looking man, but if he is grungy or dirty that turns her off. Clean appearance includes how you smell. However, let's go back even further. Clean appearance also includes where you live and what you drive. Before going out make sure your place is clean; hire a maid if you need to. On the chance a woman agrees to meet you at your place, nothing will turn her off more than visiting a dirty, unkempt house. Similarly, wash and vacuum that car.*

What is the number one mistake a man makes when approaching women?

Overly cocky attitude like he is God's gift to women.

- *Confidence is important but maintain a balance.*

What can men do that would make you more attracted to them?

Make sure he smells good on the first approach to me.

Name: Laura (married 11 years)
Age: 35
Ethnicity: Spanish

What is your perception of what women want?

An independent man, yet a good companion, one who feels love, security, someone to read their minds to know what they want without having to say it.

What kinds of guys attract you?

Physically – prefer darker skinned or George Clooney type. Sensitive, yet strong, affectionate, sexy, passionate, kinky, playful, some sense of humor, easy going, compassionate with me and others, ambitious, pursues dreams, resourceful and spontaneous.

- *With her, she is definitely attracted to the qualities of the edgy guy.*

What is the number one thing that turns you off about guys?

Inattentiveness. Smelly and bad breath. Jerk type, fake, disrespectful to others, controlling.

- *Attention and appearance of utmost importance.*

What is the number one mistake a man makes when approaching women?

When men are not authentic and overdo their attempts to talk to me. No creativity.

- *The better man approaches with his own, original creative and confident nature.*

What can men do that would make you more attracted to them?

Come off intelligently, natural conversation, authentic and show you have interest.

- *Knowledge is power, a woman wants to have a real and interesting conversation.*

Name: Isabella (single)
Age: 51
Ethnicity: Portuguese

What is your perception of what women want?

Love and consideration – that men will value them for their intrinsic qualities. A man that will maintain connection with romance, someone who will tell them beautiful things and value a woman for her intellectual qualities

What kinds of guys attract you?

An intelligent and confident man. A sports-oriented man into fitness, one with beautiful eyes that have a certain deep, sexy look, very masculine-type.

- *Notice at first her attraction is for intelligence and someone who takes care of himself. The confident man will portray that deep, sexy look and come off very masculine.*

What is the number one thing that turns you off about guys?

Vulgar type, drunk, drug users, liar, flirting while with another woman.

- *Keep attention to the one you are talking to. The confident man does not have to get drunk to make his approach nor use foul language.*

What is the number one mistake a man makes when approaching women?

Too aggressive, thinks he can get you right away.

- *Confidence is not aggression.*

What can men do that would make you more attracted to them?

He could treat me and make me feel important like calling, thinking, caring about what's going on in my life.

- *This is the emotional level that a woman desires to be treated. If you can reach that emotional level, then you may have her hooked.*

Name: Erica (married)
Age: 24
Ethnicity: Filipina

What's you perception of what women want?

Someone that makes a girl feel special and someone not ashamed or embarrassed to show affection. The man is proud to show off his woman. A man who provides security, respect, and honesty is what women want.

What kinds of guys attract you?

I like bad boys, men who take risks and Hispanic men. I'm not into the suit & tie type. Jeans, casual work boots, etc. His appearance must be strong, stands up straight, military style.

- *Notice she even used the term 'bad boy' to describe those that she is attracted to and she has attraction for the man with the strong, confident appearance.*

What is the number one thing that turns you off about guys?

Lying to try to impress me.

- *The confident man does not need to lie or exaggerate to attract a woman.*

What is the number one mistake a man makes when approaching women?

Asking right away about my relationship status. You know exactly why they are asking.

- *The confident man does not need to ask about relationship status. This will be offered to him because he has attracted the female with his confident posture, smile, and great conversation. (And even if she's taken, she may finally meet that better man she desires).*

What can men do that would make you more attracted to them?

Do not be desperate or push the issue.

- *The confident man never acts out of desperation. A female can smell the desperate man a mile a way and will make him even more desperate by ignoring him. Always come from the point of view that it is her loss for not wanting to get to know you. Of course, the better man will want to be known.*

Name: Sandy (single)
Age: 26
Ethnicity: White

What is your perception of what women want?

A man who is kind, chivalrous, sweeps her off her feet and provide that house in the suburbs with the picket fence.

What kinds of guys attract you?

A man with a great body, nice lips and has a career going for him.

- *These aspects, while they may seem physical, actually result from the confident man. A man who keeps his body in shape, keeps his appearance clean and has a successful career gives off a tremendous confident aura that is irresistible to women.*

What is the number one thing that turns you off about guys?

Someone that has an uneducated demeanor and vocabulary.

- *Remember the concept of "I was attracted to him until he opened his mouth". We can have the confident body language and smile, but if we come across as dumb, that really turns off any chance a man has to attract a female. We have let down all of the fantasies she has played in her head when we opened our mouth. The better man always has fresh things to say and does so in a way that shows his intelligence.*

What is the number one mistake a man makes when approaching women?

Someone who uses dumb ass pick up lines that I've heard for so many years now. Do guys really think that works?

- *And she is only 26, so imagine how many more dumb ass pick lines she will hear for the rest of her days. The better man doesn't use pick-up lines leave those for the amateurs. Utilize fresh, fun topics of conversation.*

What can men do that would make you more attracted to them?

Someone who can be agreeable to what I would like and not always do what he likes.

- *The confident man knows what he likes but can also be flexible to best mesh each other's desires. This is similar to the way the confident man will lead in the bedroom, a mix of what each other wants.*

Name: Elisa (married 13yrs)
Age: 41
Ethnicity: Mexican

What is your perception of what women want?

Women want happiness and security with their partner. They want to have healthy children and a man that has a career that brings in enough money (doesn't have to be rich).

What kinds of guys attract you?

Clean cut, military-style stands tall, straight and confident. Someone who is very masculine.

- *Notice like some of the women listed before, she likes the clean-cut **appearance**. A man that presents himself as the prize to be won will attract.*

What is the number one thing that turns you off about guys?

I can't stand someone who is a show-off. Especially if he's really handsome, he'll come off too cocky.

- *What women don't like about cocky guys is that the cocky guy places the woman beneath himself. **Perception is reality**, so even if that's not your intention, take care of the words you use and the attitude you give off.*

What is the number one mistake a man make when approaching women?

They assume something I'm not, like assuming that I have snotty attitude.

- *I have to say that as a 40+, she is a fine-looking woman. After meeting her, I found out what a joy it was to talk to her. Even if you approach and find out someone is married, she can be your mouthpiece for any of her available friends. This works well because you already have proof that you are someone worthwhile to know. So don't automatically dismiss conversing with a married woman.*

What can men do that would make you more attracted to them?

A man can act naturally and be himself. It can go along way to attracting.

- *In follow up conversation she mentioned that she noticed that guys pressed too much or tried to use canned pick up material when they talked to her available friends. The confident man does not need to press a female, and does not rehearse lines as if he is in a play. Conversation should come naturally and yes, practice makes perfect. The more you practice, the more natural your conversation will become.*

Name: Kajal (single)
Age: 41
Ethnicity: Indian/Hindu

What is your perception of what women want?

I think women want a man that is emotionally balanced, someone that is in middle of the continuum of being too nice to one extreme and someone who is too much of a jerk, because both sides of the continuum are dangerous. Each side will suck the life out of you. One sucks out your life with neediness and the other with deviousness. Either way you drown.

▪ *Kajal is a therapist.*

What type of guys are you attracted to?

I'm attracted to guys that are balanced as I mentioned above. I'm attracted to guys that are open to life, all experiences of life, wants to constantly change, explore, grow, revolutionize, transform, live, love, rejoice.

▪ *These are all qualities of the confident man. The nice guy will just do whatever the woman wants and will grow into something that she wants. This ultimately will repulse her because he will not stand up for himself. The jerk will only do what he wants, and will not grow with the woman, thus ultimately separating himself emotionally from her.*

What is the number one thing that turns you off about guys?

There are a couple of things that turn me off, first a guy who is cheap. He asks me out then expects me to pay half. Also, I can't stand guys that talk about, look at or text other women when they are with me. It's really trashy behavior.

- *Woman typically do not expect a lavish outing, as a matter of fact, the first outing should be something casual and not expensive. Coffee shop, happy hour drinks, pool hall, etc. It is better to go somewhere casual but fun for both of you. A lavish dinner, especially on the first date, may make a woman feel uncomfortable **as if you are expecting something at the end of the date.** Your confident demeanor, body language and smile will help the woman come to the decision that she is attracted to you and wants to kiss you (or more). As usual when you are with one woman, keep your attention on her for that two or three hour period. Yes, beautiful women will walk by you, but even Kajal admitted that a man should be discreet if he is going to sneak a peek.*

What is the number one mistake a man makes when approaching women?

A mistake a man makes is when he tries too hard and is too aggressive. Another mistake is when a man is overly friendly. It is creepy and it is obvious that he wants one thing from me.

- *The better man is not aggressive and behaves in a cool, confident manner. While sex with a woman is a goal to have, you want to make it seem like it is her idea and that she has control. Ultimately, the cool, confident man is irresistible.*

What can men do that would make you more attracted to them?

He can listen to what I have to say and ask about me instead of talking about himself. He can do what I want to do instead of always doing what he wants to do.

- *We mentioned previously listening is a requisite skill to possess and to allow the woman to do most of the talking. Interject intermittently to show that you are listening and challenge a position that a woman takes. You will do so confidently and not as a confrontation. This banter is welcomed by a woman and shows that you are a challenge. This is a powerful attractive quality.*

Name: Yvonne (single)
Age: 47
Ethnicity: White

What is your perception of what women want?

I think women want a man who is honest with them. A woman wants a man that complements her. Someone that is secure in himself and wants to spend quality time with her.

What types of guys are you attracted to?

I'm attracted to Hispanic guys with a kind of bad boy type of look. A man who is shaved bald is a great look for me. A man who dresses to impress wins me over. This person must be open to trying new things, especially in the bedroom.

- *She is attracted to someone outside her ethnic group. She is also willing to be open and have a great time. The confident man projects the fun atmosphere someone like her would be into.*

What is the number one thing that turns you off about guys?

I hate it when out with a guy that constantly looks at his phone or is texting someone while on the date. Those men never get a second chance when you break rule number one.

- *Certainly don't forget rule #1.*

What is the number one mistake a man makes when approaching women?

For me if a man comes up to me and he is dressed sloppily, I will not give him a chance. Would I be proud to stand next to someone that doesn't take care of himself when I always do.

- *She was dressed impeccably when I met her. In follow up conversations she mentioned liking a man that cared about what he wears. That was more important than if a man was good-looking or not. I actually witnessed younger guys approaching her at the lounge I was at, but these young guys had on baseball caps, shorts and sneakers. Some of them would be considered handsome yet she turned them down because she said they were sloppily dressed. To her this tells a lot about a man. As mentioned previously, appearance is a more important factor than looks.*

What can men do that would make you more attracted to them?

A man can pay attention to what I say and be attentive during conversation. And please no middle school pick up lines, I've heard them all.

- *Again, listening is a requisite skill to possess. Interject a thought to show that you are listening and challenge a position that a woman takes. NO PICK UP LINES!*

Name: Lauren (single)
Age: 24
Ethnicity: French

What is your perception of what women want?

A woman wants a hard-working man with goals that will meet them halfway in a relationship. A woman wants men who are dependable and act as a great friend.

What types of guys are you attracted to?

I like men with nice looking teeth that have a clean-cut look to them. Please no skinny jeans. As far as personality, I like someone who is funny and can take a joke.

- *Even for the younger ones, appearance is more important. So if your teeth are yellowing, bleach them. A yellow smile is a big turnoff for any age. Women also look for someone who is fun and not booooooring.*

What is the number one thing that turns you off about guys?

A big turnoff is someone who is LAZY. I may ask politely the first time, but not the second. That's when I step. Another turnoff is someone who gets jealous. Especially, a guy I just met somewhere thinks I'm his if he buys me a drink. Please…

- *First, the confident man never reacts, but acts. He remains one step ahead of the game. Secondly, it is very rare that the confident man buys a lady a drink especially upon meeting and if she asks you to. It is a test to see if you will supplicate to her and when you do, you are eliminated. Turn it around by saying that you think much better of her without having to buy her time. It's that type of challenge that women like, and you will have greater stature not just in her eyes, but in yours as well.*

What is the number one mistake a man makes when approaching women?

Men approach women as a piece of ass and much too aggressive instead of playing it smooth. They don't try to make it friendly and enjoy the company at the time.

- *The better man makes a woman feel like a human being not some piece of ass he's trying to pick up for that night. The better man will convince a woman that her ass will leave with him by the confident body language and eye contact he portrays, self-assuredness, fun conversation and attention to detail. This sounds like a bunch of things to remember especially since the newly divorced man probably hasn't been out dating in a while. Just like anything else, with practice, you will become better and natural. Heck, practice with your sisters, female cousins, friends etc.*

What can men do that would make you more attracted to them?

Men could keep themselves looking clean and definitely in shape. Doesn't have to be all big muscles and stuff. I mean not sloppily dressed or big beer gut hanging down.

- *Women seem to be much quicker than men upon a separation to get back into shape. Of course it shouldn't be that way, couples should stay in shape inside a relationship anyway to keep each other attractive. Even if you're a little older with a few 'extra pounds', women will tend to forgive if you make up for it with clean dress and appearance. They are a lot more forgiving than us guys.*

Name: Yasmeen (single)
Age: 28
Ethnicity: Arab/Muslim

What is your perception of what women want?

Women want good sex for sure. They also want the typical 'tall, dark and handsome' type; a macho man who is taller than her. Women want someone who is smart, adventurous, and creative with an educational background. Women want TLC, someone to spoil them and make the woman feel that she is the world to you.

- *So yes this is 'the' Yasmeen. Notice she perceived 'sex' as number one. I knew I liked her for a reason.*

What types of guys are you attracted to?

I like a cultured man someone with depth in thought and actions. A man who thinks critically about complex subjects and discusses them with me is very attractive.

- *I picked up on that immediately and used that to my advantage. I found her so attractive because she was not into conversing fluff like most of the 20+ year olds I have met. She is definitely more into the cognitive stimulation.*

What is the number one thing that turns you off about guys?

Someone who is cheap! Also someone who is shallow, I know he wants only one thing. Qualities like cheap and shallow are big time turnoffs.

- *Once again, if you invite, expect to pay because you are the man. Fun and interesting conversation from a confident man will likely lead to attraction. A woman will feel comfortable about sex when it is her idea.*

What is the number one mistake a man makes when approaching women?

A man approaches in such a controlling manner and thinks it's cute. He expects that I'm going to like it.

- *The jerk/bad boy is the one who tries to be too controlling.*

What can men do that would make you more attracted to them?

Be endlessly romantic and creative about it.

- *The romantic side of a man should occur once you have established a relationship with a woman. Showing romance immediately upon meeting a woman will come off creepy and needy. Moreover, don't do the same things over and over again, that gets too boring.*

Name: Kori (single)
Age: 25
Ethnicity: Arab/Christian

What is your perception of what women want?

Women want a man who is stable, funny, romantic and mature.

- *Yes this is 'the' Kori.*

What kinds of guys attract you?

I like guys who are independent and have lots of things going on in their lives. A man with ambition is a key attractive quality for me. I also like guys who are adventurous and like to go out and live life. I'm not the stay-at-home type of woman.

- *Kori is definitely into the FUN type of man, someone whom is adventurous and has a plan. To most women, nothing is sexier than a man who knows what he wants and goes after it. That's the AMBITION. I mentioned one thing I worried about was being divorced and not having enough money etc. It's a turnoff if a man stays in that situation and does nothing. It is quite a different story if you are in that situation but are actively working on trying to get out of the hellhole you are in. Women are more likely to hang around for the ride to see where it leads.*

What is the number one thing that turns you off about guys?

A man who is LAZY with no ambition is a huge turnoff to me. Of course a man who lies to try to impress me makes me go UGH!

- *It is possible that in a man's life he may suffer emotionally, physically and financially especially after a divorce. Kori implored me as I wallowed in self-pity to get out there and BE THE MAN. It doesn't matter (as much as we think) where you are in life, as along as you are on the move to improve your situation. The confident man doesn't need to lie or embellish to impress.*

What is number one mistake a man makes when approaching women?

They will portray themselves as something they are not. Many are also disrespectful.

- *A woman judges you by the respect (or lack of) that you demonstrate upon meeting her. It is not even about her necessarily, but how you treat others as well. She will judge your treatment of servers, her friends, etc. The better man treats all others with respect.*

What can men do that would make you more attracted to them?

He needs to make me feel like he is not guaranteed to me. That way, I will be on my best to keep him close.

- *We mentioned earlier, women like challenges. If you show your all to a woman upon meeting her, what challenge is left for her? You become predictable and boring. Give enough to attract her and leave enough mystery for subsequent meetings. This way she will remain interested to find out more about you. Mystery and challenge are two great attraction strategies.*

OTHER COMMENTS

Sarah Liz (30, Mexican, in a relationship) – A woman would like a man that looks like a bad boy but really is a nice guy inside.

Jaya (41, Yugoslavian, single) – Go where the love is and not *where you think it should be.*

Ilka (38, Puerto Rican, married 15 years) - Not so sure that women are attracted to bad boys as much as they are just bored with guys that are too predictable. Only the stupid women stay with jerks instead of seeking intelligent and successful men.

Hazel (41, Nicaraguan, single) - Bad boys are fun... but ONLY for a little while. That doesn't last very long.
Jennifer (45, Filipina, single) – I get attracted to bad boys, but that lasts a short time.

8

Conclusion

AS MENTIONED PREVIOUSLY, this book details my struggles in handling life after crisis relationships. I am a regular man that dealt with the misconceptions that I had about myself and how others would perceive me. At a recent conference I went to I heard a statistic that 90% of the things that manifest in our lives do so because of the subconscious beliefs in ourselves. This cannot be understated because WE have the power within us to succeed in any aspect of our lives. WE are the ultimate limiting factor for ourselves. Coming out of the divorce and later the separation with Yasmeen, I was the one that had a limited outlook about myself. Since I kept that with me subconsciously, this manifested outwardly in the way I looked, talked and interacted with others. Kori helped me change my beliefs within and this new outlook also manifested itself in the way I looked, talked and interacted with others.

Even with these new beliefs at times doubts, fears, and other negative feelings jump out at you when you least expect it. One time, I became perturbed about not hearing from a woman after contacting her a couple of times.

Kori immediately put me in check.

"Back it up, needy boy. You don't want to show that you need her to make you happy through out the day. If she calls, great, if not, you have others numbers. If she's not interested, that's on her not you."

It's a wonderful feeling to have a friend like Kori whom is willing to tell it to me like it is. The women I have spoken to admit that good men are in short supply. Scrutinize the way men are portrayed on television, as buffoons and idiots. Sometimes we forget that as cool, confident males, *WE are the ones in demand.* However, many men don't show that true masculinity that women desire. In business it is said 'build it and they will come'. Similarly, build that masculinity and they will come. Developing masculinity is a lifelong endeavor and changes over time. However, there are certain core characteristics that women say are missing from today's men.

In follow up discussions with the women I interviewed, contemporary men are missing some valuable qualities that would make them more attractive such as: chivalry, honesty, respect, and value for the woman. Both Kori and Yasmeen mentioned chivalry as the number one thing missing from men.

At first glance these would seem as qualities of the 'nice guy', however in reality these are the characteristics of the better man. A better man would open the door for a female, be up front, and show deference and reverence for her. All of this can be done while maintaining a man's own dignity and this strongly attracts a woman that wants a true *man*, someone that can give her what she wants while knowing he is of high quality. The 'nice guy' may perform similar deeds, however, he does so to his detriment. He gives away too much of his own power and that places him on a supplicating level thus emasculating himself and invariably repulsing a woman. The 'bad boy' or 'jerk' cares only about himself and may not see the need to treat a female properly and thus this is done to her detriment. Again, the jerk attraction is very limited and the relationship can be volatile which no confident man needs to live with.

As a divorced man, it is likely you have children to care for; your children do not need to be around volatile relationships. Your children look up to you, you wouldn't want your son behaving in a supplicating or jerky manner nor would you want your daughters behaving in a desperate, volatile manner. A common mistake people make after a divorce or separation is to bring other girlfriends or boyfriends around their children. I do not suggest this and would only introduce another woman to my children if my intention were to engage her (for me right now, there is absolutely no need to think engagement and marriage). Your children should see you as 'dad' and not some 'playa'. It is not something endearing for your daughter to see, she will intrinsically see herself as just another object in men's eyes. I challenge any father that truly wants that for *his* daughter. Boys should be taught from their confident fathers how to present themselves in a confident manner emulating the best part of being a man. Boys should also be taught to treat girls as human beings. Moreover, your personal life, what you do on your weekends off is YOUR business and should not be advertised to the children.

As we go through our daily lives, we will continue to make mistakes. The important part is to learn from them and make the next interaction successful. Recently, I made a mistake of NOT approaching a woman even though she was obviously interested in meeting. I guess some old anxieties jumped out at me. I realized later what a huge mistake that was as I reread what *I had written herein*. Laugh at yourself and move on to make the next situation a success. The other part of meeting people is to HAVE FUN with it. If you put too much pressure on yourself such as saying "oh I have to meet someone tonight", the desperation will manifest itself and women are able to smell the desperation, neediness and emasculation. If your are not having fun, then it becomes as much of a chore as that job you hate waking up to every morning. Happy hour is supposed to be just that – happy and fun.

Let's remember (me included) the requisite qualities of that edgy, confident, better man:

ATTRACTION
a. <u>Confidence</u> - #1 attraction quality.
b. <u>Fun/Spontaneity</u> – keep it light, not too much pressure on yourself or the people you are trying to meet. DO YOUR HOMEWORK, keep abreast (figuratively and literally) of current events in your community.
c. <u>Clean and polished appearance</u> – more important than just being good-looking.
d. <u>Masterfully Conversant</u> – Tease and challenge a woman in a fun atmosphere and use humor to your advantage. If you're not sure how to use humor, watch some stand-up comedians. You must also display your intelligence by learning new things to make yourself worldly and worthy of meeting because knowledge is power. Avoid spouting statistics or giving advice.

AVOID NEGATIVE BODY LANGUAGE
a. Keep confident upright posture
b. Smile and other positive facial expressions
c. Keep hands out of your pockets and steer clear of folded arms in front of you.
d. Maintain eye contact with the person you are talking to and DO NOT STARE at certain body parts or other women (discretion).

I have chosen every word for this book carefully and I have avoided giving too many specific words for your interactions. Meeting other people should come from within and that results in enhanced feelings about yourself rather than rehearsing canned material. A famous army general once said "scrap any plans once the war begins." If you rehearse canned material, you will be thrown off and frustrated once a distraction happens or the meeting does not go as planned. That's why it is more important as women say to 'be yourself', the confident self. A modern day rapper said "everybody dies but not many people live". After a divorce or separation, this is the opportunity to live again and start anew a social life with different, exciting possibilities." Remember more than 3.5 billion women worldwide!

- **NOTE:** Just before the editing process, I received a phone call from Yasmeen! She said she is back in the U.S. for good (no promises or anything). Holy crap, after everything had been going well for me, all of those feelings, hopes, and desires came back to me. Damn, what do I do? Try to reignite what we had before or just leave our romance in the past? Kori warned me to tread carefully and handle my feelings. It feels extremely comforting to have her on the battlefield with me.

Oh well, scrap the plans and let the war begin!

- **NOTE 2:** If you are in the Los Angeles area and desiring a safe way get a golden tan check out:

Soleil Custom Tanning
(818)438-1761

www.ingramcontent.com/pod-product-compliance
Lightning Source LLC
Chambersburg PA
CBHW031245280526
45784CB00004B/1724